FRENCH

STANDARD GRADE COURSE NOTES

JANE RENTON
Principal Teacher of French
Beath High School, Cowdenbeath

AND

PATRICIA THOMSON
Principal Teacher of Modern Languages
Glenwood High School, Glenrothes

Published by Leckie & Leckie
8 Whitehill Terrace
St Andrews KY16 8RN
Tel. 01334 - 475656
Fax. 01334 - 477392

Edited by Iain Hirschfeld

Special thanks to the production team:
Mary Ambrose, Julie Barclay,
Nolan Cocker, Alison Irving,
Susanna Kirk, Bruce Ryan,
Emma Saint-Val and
Hamish Sanderson;

the speakers on the tape: Stuart Burt (former pupil at Beath High School), Lara Ferguson (pupil at Glenwood High School), Anne Guénerie (French Assistant at Beath High School) and Patricia Thomson;

the Scottish Examination Board for their kind permission to reproduce past examination questions. (Some questions have been adapted. Answers do not emanate from the Board.)

ISBN 1-898890-60-9
A CIP Catalogue record for this book is available from the British Library.

WITH AUDIO CASSETTE

Leckie & Leckie

Contents

1. Introduction

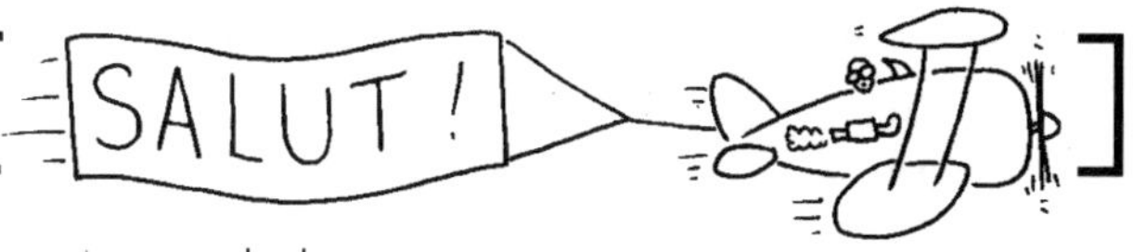

The aims of these *Course Notes* and accompanying *tape* are to help you:

- familiarise yourself with the elements of *Standard Grade French*
- develop and practise all the necessary skills
- organise your work throughout the course
- revise effectively for the exam.

It is impossible to cover all the aspects of your course in these *Notes* and *tape* but you will find that the major ones have been covered.

The ***Course Notes*** are divided up according to the skill areas:

- **Speaking**
  - useful words and phrases (with their pronunciations on the tape)
  - three Speaking tests of varying levels of difficulty
    - how to prepare for them
    - a possible version of each test printed (and read out on the tape)
- **Reading**
  - hints on how to tackle the Reading exam at Foundation, General and Credit Levels using past exam questions
  - dictionary skills
- **Listening**
  - how to concentrate on key question words
  - the importance of vocabulary (including **faux amis**)
  - the importance of numbers
  - other hints for the Listening exam
- **Writing**
  - hints for effective writing
  - General Level Writing
    - writing about yourself
    - writing notes
    - writing postcards
  - how to plan and write a Credit Level essay
- **Grammar**
  - nouns
  - verbs
    - present tense
    - perfect tense
    - immediate future tense
    - reflexive verbs
  - adjectives
  - asking questions
  - impressive phrases

The accompanying ***tape*** is designed to help you develop your Speaking and Listening skills. It is divided into ten sections. Each section helps you in a different way. For example, sometimes you will practise your Listening skills by listening to French on the tape and answering questions printed in the *Course Notes*. At other times you will practise your Speaking skills by listening carefully to French phrases on the tape and then repeating them aloud as you hear each one. Follow the instructions at the start of each section on the tape. They tell you what to do in each section.

When you see the tape symbol in the book, be ready to listen to the tape.

When you get to the end of each section, rewind the tape to the beginning of the section and listen to it again. Listen carefully to each section several times. This will help you perform well in Standard Grade French.

All the French on the tape is spoken by a native French speaker, except sections 2 and 5 and the end of section 10. These are spoken by Scottish students to make them realistic.

Throughout the *Course Notes* there are exercises to help you practise what you have learnt.

When you see the exercise symbol in the *Course Notes*, be ready to do an exercise. Some of the exercises are designed to be done right away to help you practise what you have just learnt. Other exercises are designed to be done throughout your Standard Grade French course.

Where appropriate, you will find answers to exercises (and transcripts of exercises on the tape) at the end of each chapter.

2. Speaking

Speaking is a **very important** skill: it is worth 50% of the marks for Standard Grade French.

During your 4th year, you will be tested up to six times in Speaking:

- The tests will take different forms, including speaking

  - with a partner
  - with your teacher
  - in a group
  - onto a cassette.

- You may be speaking either

  - as yourself, e.g. telling your teacher about your future plans or
  - playing a role, e.g. imagining you are on holiday in France and booking into a campsite.

Useful words and phrases

The list below will help you prepare for all sorts of Speaking tests. Under each of the 18 headings recommended in the Standard Grade syllabus are a number of useful words and phrases.

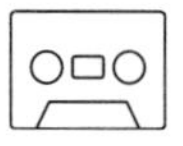

Listen to **section one** of the tape for the correct pronunciation. After you hear each French phrase on the tape, repeat it aloud to yourself trying to imitate the pronunciation.

- **Greetings**

  - **Bonjour!** – Hello! / Good morning! / Good afternoon!
  - **Salut!** – Hi!
  - **Bonsoir!** – Good evening!

- **Taking leave**

  - **Au revoir!** – Goodbye!
  - **À bientôt!** – See you soon!
  - **Bonne nuit!** – Good night!

- **Attracting attention**

  - **Excusez-moi!** / **Pardon!** – Excuse me!
  - **Monsieur!** – Sir!
  - **Madame!** – Miss!

- **Introducing someone**

  - **Voici ...** This is ...
  - **Je te présente ...** / **Je vous présente ...** – May I introduce ...

- **Expressing good wishes**

  - **Bon anniversaire!**
    Happy Birthday!
  - **Bonne année!**
    Happy New Year!
  - **Bon appétit!**
    Enjoy your meal!

- **Thanking**

  - **Merci.**
    Thank you.
  - **Merci beaucoup.**
    Thank you very much.
  - **Je vous remercie.**
    Thank you. (formal)

- **Apologising**

  - Je m'excuse.
  - Je regrette.
  - Je suis désolé.

  } I'm sorry.

- **Agreeing**

  - C'est ça! — That's right! / That's it!
  - D'accord! — OK!
  - Tu as raison! — You're right!

- **Disagreeing**

  - Tu parles!
    You must be joking!
  - Je ne suis pas d'accord!
    I don't agree with that!
  - Ce n'est pas vrai!
    That's not true!
  - Surtout pas!
    Certainly not!

- **Accepting**

  - Je veux bien. — I'd like that.
  - Bonne idée! — Good idea!
  - Chouette! — Great!

- **Refusing**

  - Non merci.
    No thanks.
  - Je ne veux pas.
    I don't want to.
  - Ça ne me dit rien.
    I don't fancy that.

- **Coping with language problems**

  - Je n'ai pas compris.
    I didn't understand.
  - Répétez, s'il vous plaît?
    Can you repeat, please?
  - Vous pouvez parler plus lentement?
    Can you speak more slowly?

- **Opinions/Feelings**

  - C'est délicieux!
    That's delicious!
  - Quelle barbe!
    What a bore!
  - Quelle jolie maison!
    What a pretty house!

- **Likes/Dislikes/Reasons**
  - J'aime l'EPS parce que je suis fort(e) en sport.
    I like PE because I'm good at sport.
  - Je n'aime pas le coca – c'est trop sucré.
    I don't like cola – it's too sweet.
  - J'adore les hamsters – ils sont tellement mignons.
    I love hamsters – they're so cute.

- **Needs/Requests**
  - Je voudrais deux billets pour Bordeaux.
    I'd like two tickets for Bordeaux.
  - Vous avez de la moutarde?
    Do you have any mustard?
  - J'ai besoin d'une chambre pour la nuit.
    I need a room for the night.
  - Un coca, s'il vous plaît.
    A cola, please.

- **Intentions**
  - Je vais quitter l'école en juin.
    I'm going to leave school in June.
  - J'ai l'intention d'aller à l'université.
    I intend to go to university.
  - J'ai envie de visiter le Japon.
    I want to visit Japan.

- **Permission**
  - Puis-je te parler un moment?
    May I speak to you for a moment?
  - Est-ce que je peux sortir ce soir?
    May I go out this evening?

- **Inviting/Suggesting**
  - Tu veux aller au cinéma?
    Do you want to go to the cinema?
  - Tu viens chez moi pour Noël?
    Are you coming to my home at Christmas?
  - On boit quelque chose?
    Shall we have something to drink?

Throughout your Standard Grade course, work on the following exercise.

Exercise 1

Make a note of any other useful words and phrases you meet.

Now work through these three role-plays to practise using some of these useful words and phrases:

Telephone role-play

Try this pupil/teacher role-play, studying the hints to help you with it:

Exercise 2

You phone your French pen-pal to arrange an outing to the cinema. (Your teacher plays the role of your French pen-pal.)

1. **Look through** the list on pages 4 and 5. **Pick out** the headings and some useful words and phrases you will need for this role-play.
2. Next, make up a **plan** using the headings you have chosen, like the example below.
3. To complete the task, make sure you also:
   - ask/state facts about what time the film starts
   - arrange where and when to meet.
4. Finally, **listen** to this role-play on **section two** of the tape. The transcript is on page 9.

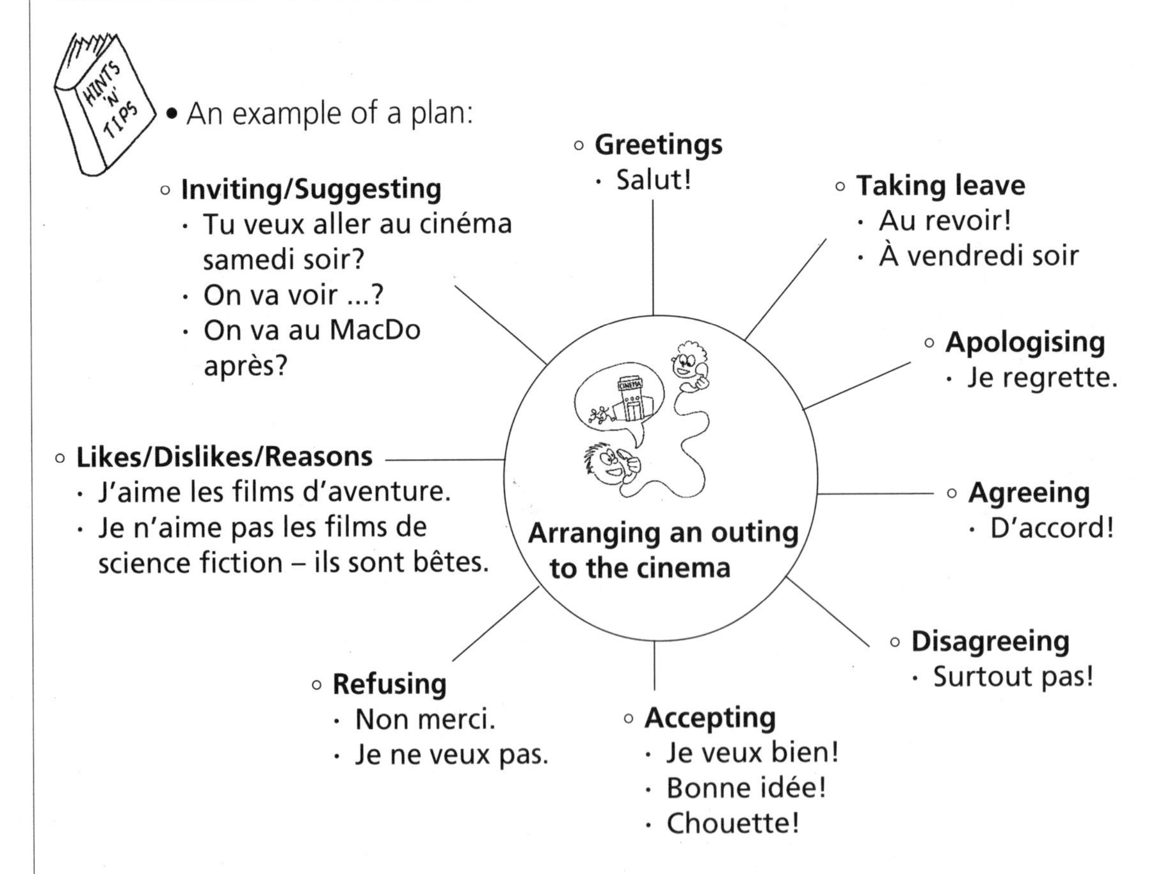
HINTS 'N' TIPS
• An example of a plan:
Arranging an outing to the cinema
○ Greetings
· Salut!
○ Taking leave
· Au revoir!
· À vendredi soir
○ Apologising
· Je regrette.
○ Agreeing
· D'accord!
○ Disagreeing
· Surtout pas!
○ Accepting
· Je veux bien!
· Bonne idée!
· Chouette!
○ Refusing
· Non merci.
· Je ne veux pas.
○ Likes/Dislikes/Reasons
· J'aime les films d'aventure.
· Je n'aime pas les films de science fiction – ils sont bêtes.
○ Inviting/Suggesting
· Tu veux aller au cinéma samedi soir?
· On va voir ...?
· On va au MacDo après?

- Remember that the list of useful words and phrases is only a starting point. It cannot provide all you need for every Speaking test.
- Remember also that your teacher may not always say what you expect.
  For example, in this task, he or she may not be able to go on the day or at the time you suggest. Be prepared for this!

Tourist role-play

Try this pupil/teacher role-play, studying the hints to help you with it:

Exercise 3

You go into the tourist office in a French town to find out what there is to do and to get accommodation. (Your teacher plays the role of the Tourist Officer.)

1. Once again, **look through** the list on pages 4 and 5. **Pick out** the headings and some words and phrases which will be useful. Notice that you may have to change some of the words to suit the topic of the exercise.
2. Next, make a **plan** like the one below.
3. Look at the other hints below to help you with other vocabulary you will need.
4. Finally, **listen** to this role-play on **section two** of the tape. The transcript is on page 9.

- An example of a plan:

Finding out about town and getting accommodation

- **Greetings**
  - Bonjour, Madame/Monsieur.
- **Thanking**
  - Merci, Monsieur/Madame.
- **Refusing**
  - Non merci.
  - Ça ne me dit rien.
- **Coping with language problems**
  - Répétez, s'il vous plaît.
- **Opinions/Feelings**
  - C'est parfait!
- **Likes/Dislikes**
  - Je n'aime pas le sport.
  - Je préfère l'histoire.
  - Je n'aime pas beaucoup le bruit.
- **Needs/Requests**
  - Vous avez un plan de la ville et des brochures?
  - J'ai besoin d'une chambre pour la nuit.
- **Intentions**
  - J'ai l'intention de visiter le château.
  - Je vais partir demain.

- You will also need to know:
  - **Tourist Office Vocabulary**

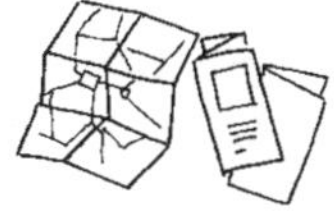

- un plan de la ville — a town plan
- des brochures — some brochures
- un dépliant — a leaflet
- Qu'est-ce qu'il y a à voir ici? — What is there to see here?
- Qu'est-ce qu'il y a à faire ici? — What is there to do here?

Opening and Closing Times

- Il/Elle ouvre à quelle heure? — What time does it open?
- Il/Elle ferme à quelle heure? — What time does it close?

Hotel Vocabulary

- une nuit — one night
- un quartier tranquille — a quiet area
- réserver une chambre — to book a room

- You should also decide in advance what your **preferences** are:
  - what you'd like to do while visiting the town
  - what sort of accommodation you'd like.

School role-play

Try this pupil/pupil role-play, studying the hints to help you with it:

Exercise 4

You and your partner have a conversation about the differences between school in Scotland and school in France. You are the Scottish pupil and your partner plays the role of a French pupil. The French pupil is provided with the following details:

- Lycée René Descartes, Perpignan
- situé en centre ville
- 1000 élèves
- Les cours { commencent à 8h. / finissent à 17h.

Matières étudiées
mathématiques
sciences physiques
anglais
espagnol
histoire/géographie
français

1. Make up a **plan** like the one below to help you talk about your own school.
2. Ask questions about your partner's school in France.
3. Use some expressions of acknowledgement and surprise (see below).
4. Finally, **listen** to this conversation on **section two** of the tape. The transcript is on page 9.

- An example of a plan:

Stating facts about your school

- **Name of your school**
  - Mon école s'appelle ...
- **Where the school is situated**
  - Elle se trouve dans ...
- **How many pupils**
  - Il y a ... élèves environ.
- **How you travel to school**
  - J'y vais à pied.
- **Starting and finishing times**
  - Les cours commencent à ... et finissent à ...
- **How many periods a day**
  - On a ... cours de ... minutes par jour.
- **Likes/Dislikes/Reasons**
  - J'adore ..., c'est ...
- **Homework**
  - Je passe ... heures chaque soir à faire mes devoirs.
- **How long you've been there**
  - J'y suis depuis ... ans.
- **General impressions**
  - À mon avis, l'école est ...

- Pages 44–47 will help you form the questions you will need to ask your partner.
- Here are some expressions of acknowledgement and surprise:
  - Ah bon? — Really?
  - C'est vrai? — Is that so?
  - Ça m'étonne. — That surprises me.

Transcripts

Telephone role-play

You Salut, Jean. C'est Lara à l'appareil. Tu veux aller au cinéma samedi soir?
Teacher Je regrette, je ne suis pas libre samedi soir.
You Alors, si on y allait vendredi soir?
Teacher Oui, d'accord. Je veux bien.
You On va voir 'La Planète Noire'? C'est un film de science fiction.
Teacher Surtout pas! Je n'aime pas les films de science fiction – ils sont bêtes!
You Alors, on va voir le film d'aventure à l'Odéon?
Teacher D'accord. J'aime les films d'aventure.
You On va au MacDo après?
Teacher Oui, d'accord. Bonne idée!
You Chouette! Le film commence à huit heures. Rendez-vous à huit heures moins le quart devant le cinéma?
Teacher D'accord.
You À vendredi soir, alors. Au revoir.
Teacher Au revoir, Lara.

Tourist role-play

You Bonjour, Madame. Vous avez un plan de la ville et des brochures?
Teacher Bien sûr! Voilà! Vous voulez aussi un dépliant sur le centre sportif?
You Non merci. Je n'aime pas le sport – ça ne me dit rien. Je préfère l'histoire – qu'est-ce qu'il y a à voir ici?
Teacher Eh bien, il y a le château.
You Oui, j'ai l'intention de visiter le château. Il ouvre à quelle heure?
Teacher À dix heures du matin – mais prenez ce dépliant, Monsieur.
You Merci. En plus, j'ai besoin d'une chambre pour la nuit.
Teacher Il y a un très bon hôtel en centre ville.
You Ah non, je n'aime pas beaucoup le bruit.
Teacher Alors, il y a l'Hôtel Bon Séjour.
You Répétez, s'il vous plaît.
Teacher L'Hôtel Bon Séjour. B-o-n S-é-j-o-u-r.
You Il se trouve dans un quartier tranquille?
Teacher Oui, très tranquille.
You C'est parfait! Vous pouvez téléphoner pour résérver une chambre de ma part?
Teacher Bien sûr. C'est pour combien de nuits?
You Une nuit seulement. Je vais partir demain.
Teacher Très bien. Je téléphone tout de suite.
You Merci, Madame.

School role-play

You Bonjour, Stuart. Tu peux me parler de ton école en France?
Partner Eh bien, mon école s'appelle Lycée Descartes. Elle se trouve dans le centre de Perpignan.
You Il y a combien d'élèves?
Partner Oh, c'est une grande école – il y a mille élèves environ.
You Comment est-ce que tu vas à l'école?
Partner D'habitude j'y vais à pied mais quand il pleut, je prends le bus.
You Les cours commencent à quelle heure? C'est comme en Écosse, je suppose?
Partner Les cours commencent à huit heures.
You Ah bon? Ici on commence à neuf heures moins le quart.
Partner Tu as de la chance! Et les cours finissent à quelle heure?
You À trois heures et demie.
Partner Chez nous c'est plus tard. On finit à cinq heures.
You Quelle horreur! Et combien de cours est-ce que tu as par jour?
Partner Nous avons huit cours de cinquante-cinq minutes. Et en Écosse?
You Nous, on a huit cours de quarante minutes.
Partner Quelle est ta matière préférée?
You J'adore l'informatique – c'est amusant et pratique pour la vie active.
Partner Tu as beaucoup de devoirs?
You Oh, pas mal. Je passe deux heures en moyenne à faire mes devoirs chaque soir.
Partner C'est quand même moins qu'en France.
You Depuis quand est-ce que tu vas à ton école?
Partner Je suis en seconde – c'est ma première année au lycée.
You Je suis en quatrième année.
Partner Alors, tu préfères l'école en France ou en Écosse?
You Moi, je préfère l'école en Écosse. Je ne voudrais pas travailler jusqu'à cinq heures.

3. Reading

Hints

Here are some hints to help you do well in the Reading exam:

- Pace yourself – don't run out of time.
- Read all of the French, including the title.
- Don't assume you will get the correct answer by writing what is in the picture.
- Read the questions carefully and make sure you know what you are being asked.
- Look at how many marks each question is worth – this will help you to decide how much you should write.

- You won't have time to look up every word in the dictionary. Decide which are the key words.
- Check your answers! After you have written your answers, go back and read over your work. Check that your answers are written in English (unless your answer is a French place name which you cannot translate). Check also that you have not left any gaps. Have a guess if you have to – your guess just might be correct.

- Remember to revise your vocabulary throughout your Standard Grade course. The more words you know, the less you will have to look up in the dictionary. This will save you time in the exam.

Foundation Level

Try exercises 5 and 6. Read the hints to help you answer the questions. Remember you will probably need your dictionary too.

Exercise 5

You read a review of a film:

L'ENFANT-LION

Un petit garçon africain et une lionne ... Ils sont amis. Mais un jour ils sont séparés par des hommes. C'est une formidable aventure. Patrick Grandperret a mis cinq ans pour réaliser ce film.

	Marks
1. There are two main characters in the film. Who are they?	**(2)**
2. What happens to them?	**(1)**
3. Do you think Patrick Grandperret is the director, an actor or the stuntman?	**(1)**

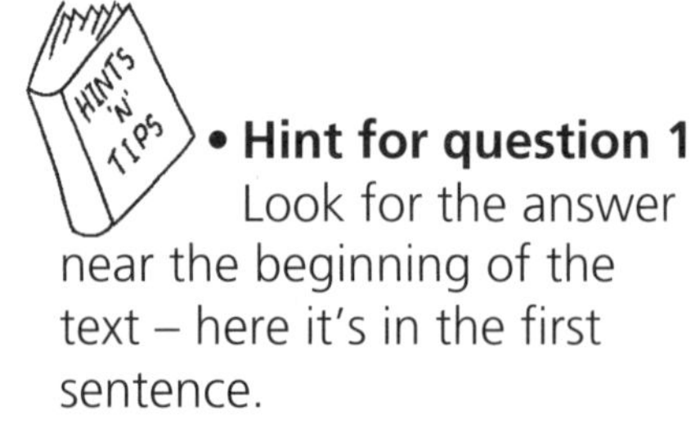

- **Hint for question 1**
  Look for the answer near the beginning of the text – here it's in the first sentence.
- **Hint for question 2**
  There are two key words – both are similar to the English.
- **Hint for question 3**
  The last sentence is about Patrick Grandperret. Look up **réaliser** to find the answer.

Exercise 6

While camping in France, you pick up a few brochures in the camp office. This unusual restaurant catches your attention:

Unique dans notre région!!!

La Crêperie panoramique du Château d'Eau

POUR Y MONTER, UN ASCENSEUR.

OUVERT

en saison: fin mars à fin septembre, de 10 H à 23 H (service des repas de 12 H 00 à 22 H 30) sans interruption.

Marks

1. What are the restaurant's two specialities? **(2)**
2. How do you get to the top of the tower? **(1)**
3. When is it open? Tick (✔) **one** box only. **(1)**

Mid-March to mid-September	
End of March to end of September	
End of March to mid-September	

4. What are the opening times of the tower? Tick (✔) **one** box. **(1)**

10 o'clock in the morning until 11 o'clock at night	
12 noon until 10.30 at night	

- **Hint for question 1** There is only one place where there are clearly two words on their own. Look them up in your dictionary if you don't know them.
- **Hint for question 2** There is a picture of the top of the tower. Read the five words directly underneath it and you will find the answer.
- **Hint for question 3** Find the bit in the text where two months are mentioned. You may have to look up **fin**.
- **Hint for question 4** There are two opening and closing times mentioned. The times in the brackets refer to **service des repas**. Look up **repas** in your dictionary. Is this what you're looking for?

General Level

Now try exercises 7 and 8. Remember to read the hints before answering the questions.

Exercise 7

You read about a group of young people who are going to spend a very unusual year:

UNE ANNÉE SCOLAIRE PAS COMME LES AUTRES

Le 3 octobre, un groupe de jeunes Françaises et Français, âgés de 14 à 15 ans, va embarquer pour un tour du monde, accompagné de Jean-Pierre, l'animateur de l'association, *Les enfants du voyage*.

«J'ai envie de voyager, de voir comment les gens vivent dans d'autres pays du monde,» explique Yohann, un membre du groupe. «Et c'est bon pour apprendre des langues!»

Marks

1. This school year will be very unusual for the young people in the article. Explain why. **(1)**
2. Why is Yohann looking forward to this school year? Mention **two** things. **(2)**

- You will find the answer to question 1 in the first paragraph and the answer to question 2 in the second paragraph.
- To answer question 1, ignore all the information about people, their ages and their jobs. This leaves you with the phrase **va embarquer pour un tour du monde**. Look up **monde** and see if you can work out the answer.
- To answer question 2, you have a choice of three things. Probably the two easiest are: **envie de voyager** and **c'est bon pour apprendre des langues**.
  Look up **envie** and **apprendre** and you should be able to work out the answer. Can you find the third option for yourself?
- Notice that the picture has not helped you in any way to understand this text.

Exercise 8

Read this article which gives advice on recording animal and bird calls:

Silence! On enregistre

Une autre activité intéressante: tu peux enregistrer les cris.

Tu as besoin simplement d'un appareil à cassettes ordinaires et d'un micro.

Il y a deux simples précautions à prendre.

- Choisis un lieu calme – pas d'autoroute à proximité, par exemple.
- Essaie de trouver un animal ou un oiseau qui n'est pas trop entouré par d'autres animaux.

Marks

You are told to pay attention to **two** things when recording. What are they? **(2)**

- Although this text looks quite long, you do not need to understand a large part of it. You are asked to find two points and there are two dots (·) at the end section of the text. This is where you should look for your answer.
- The key phrases are **un lieu calme** and **un animal ou un oiseau ... pas trop entouré par d'autres animaux.**
- Notice the word **pas** in the second phrase. Remember that **pas** means 'not'.

Credit Level

- In the Credit Reading Paper you can expect to have to read quite lengthy pieces of French. Do not panic – remember you do not have to understand every word!
- Always **use the questions as a guide** to what to look for in the passage.
- You can **expect the questions to be in order**, i.e. question 1 will be about the beginning of the text and so on.

Read through exercise 9. Study the hints and then try to answer the questions.

Exercise 9

While on holiday in France, you buy a magazine. The first article you read is about the actress, Marlène Jobert, and her two daughters.

« Je vis constamment dans la peur »

Chaque soir, le rituel est le même: les jumelles, Eva et Joy, s'allongent devant la cheminée, et leur maman, Marlène Jobert, la célèbre actrice, raconte une de ses histoires. Pour les filles, c'est le moment le plus tendre de la journée.

Mais, une fois les filles couchées, Marlène s'inquiète. «Je suis célèbre. Voilà pourquoi je suis très angoissée ... j'ai peur ... si un fou enlevait mes filles, ou cherchait à leur faire du mal», dit-elle.

Si Marlène Jobert est très maternelle, c'est peut-être à cause de son enfance difficile. «J'étais l'aînée de cinq enfants. Nous étions pauvres. Mon père était très sévère. Si je suis devenue actrice, c'est peut-être parce que le seul moyen d'échapper aux tristes weekends en famille, c'était le théâtre.» Son père a insisté pour que Marlène soit placée dans une classe trop avancée pour elle. «C'est à partir de ce moment que je me suis mise à détester l'école. Aujourd'hui encore, je suis complexée à cause de mon manque de culture. Comme je suis insomniaque, je lis beaucoup la nuit. Ça me permet de rattraper un peu le retard.»

Eva et Joy, elles, connaissent beaucoup plus de tendresse. Si Marlène a renoncé à sa carrière pendant quelque temps, c'est pour passer le plus de temps possible avec elles. Et c'est à force d'inventer des histoires pour endormir ses deux filles que l'actrice s'est prise de passion pour l'écriture. «J'ai essayé la chanson, mais pardessus tout je préfère écrire pour enfants.» Elle a même découvert une nouvelle carrière, car elle a publié trois livres pour enfants, avec des cassettes pour les très jeunes.

Exercise 9 (cont.)

		Marks
1.	In Marlène Jobert's house, what is the evening ritual?	**(2)**
2.	What does Marlène Jobert fear might happen to her daughters?	**(2)**
3.	Marlène Jobert had a difficult childhood. Give any **three** pieces of information about it.	**(3)**
4.	What caused Marlène to dislike school?	**(1)**
5.	Why has Marlène given up her job as an actress for the time being?	**(1)**
6.	**(a)** What work does Marlène do now that she is no longer acting?	**(1)**
	(b) What success has she had so far?	**(1)**

HINTS 'N' TIPS

- Question 1 asks you about Marlène Jobert's 'evening ritual'. In the first line of the text you see the word **soir** which you know means 'evening' and the word **rituel** which is easy to guess.
  The question is worth two marks, so look in the first paragraph for two points in answer to the question.
  You have to find out what the two daughters do in the evening and what their mother does.
  Always aim to look up as few words as possible in your dictionary. In this case your maximum is three!
- In question 2 the key word is 'fear'. What is the French for 'fear'? Look it up in your dictionary if you need to. Can you find it in paragraph 2?
  Now find the two things she fears. Maximum number of words to look up is three!
- Now look at questions 3 and 4. The answers for both of these questions are in paragraph three.
  Where should you stop looking for the answer to question 3 and start looking for the answer to question 4?
  Can you find three things that were difficult about her childhood? Maximum number of words to look up is two!
  Can you find what caused her to dislike school? You shouldn't have to look up anything here!
- For question 5, first think of another word for 'job' in English. Did you think of 'career'?
  Now look for a similar word in French and you'll find the French for 'give up her job'. The answer is in the same sentence.
- For question 6 (a), find references in paragraph four to what Marlène likes – there are two words you should recognise. In this way you should find the answer.
  Find the answer to question 6 (b) in the final sentence.

Check your answers to exercises 5 to 9 by looking at page 18.

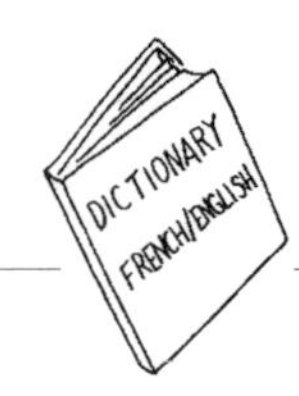

Using your French dictionary

You may use a dictionary in both your **Reading** and **Writing** exams.

But beware! Although a dictionary is helpful, there can be drawbacks in using it. Here are a few hints:

- From the start of your Standard Grade course, get to know your dictionary well. It's preferable to use the same dictionary throughout your Standard Grade course so you are able to find things quickly and easily.
  Be aware of some common dictionary abbreviations, including:
  n = noun, *m* = masculine, *f* = feminine (often combined as *nm* or *nf*)
  pl = plural
  vt or *vi* = verb
  adj = adjective
- Do not assume that the first meaning you find for a word is the right one. Look further until you find a meaning which makes sense of what you're reading.
- In the Reading and Writing exams do not overuse your dictionary, e.g. don't look up words you know 'just in case'. Do not look up words with obvious English equivalents.
- You won't have time in your Reading Paper to look up every word. In any case, there are many words you would not find – for example, parts of an irregular verb.
- In the Writing Paper try to write what you know in French. Do not think in English and then use your dictionary to translate.

Read through exercise 10. However, before attempting to answer the two questions study all the hints on page 17. The hints will help you pinpoint the words you need to look up. (Check your answers by looking at page 18.)

Exercise 10

Emballé
C'est mangé!

Bientôt, quand tu manges des frites dans la rue, tu vas aussi manger l'emballage! Un Australien a inventé un cornet de frites en pomme de terre qui se mange comme un cornet de glace.
Les emballages qui traînent par terre – c'est fini.

Marks

1. Which Australian invention is talked about? **(1)**
2. How will this invention help the environment? **(1)**

The meaning of most sentences depends on **nouns** and **verbs**, so nouns and verbs are the most important words to look up.

- What is a noun?
  A noun is the name of a person or thing, e.g. 'mother', 'Jack', 'telephone' and 'health'.

So, a noun will often follow:

- words for 'the': **le/la/l'/les**
- words for 'a': **un/une**
- words for 'some': **du/de la/de l'/des**
- possessives:
  - **mon/ma/mes** – my
  - **ton/ta/tes** – your
  - **son/sa/ses** – his/her
  - **notre/nos** – our
  - **votre/vos** – your
  - **leur/leurs** – their

For more information about nouns, study the Grammar section on page 38.

- The nouns in the text are underlined below:

Emballé
C'est mangé!

Bientôt, quand tu manges des frites dans la rue, tu vas aussi manger l'emballage! Un Australien a inventé un cornet de frites en pomme de terre qui se mange comme un cornet de glace.
Les emballages qui traînent par terre – c'est fini.

- Which of these will you need to look up?
  - probably **emballage** and **cornet**.

- What is a verb?
  A verb is a doing or being word, e.g. 'sell', 'hold', 'is' and 'find'.

A verb will often follow:

- a subject pronoun:
  - **je** – I
  - **tu** – you
  - **il** – he
  - **elle** – she
  - **on** – we
  - **nous** – we
  - **vous** – you
  - **ils** – they
  - **elles** – they
- **qui** – who
- the name of a person or thing

For more information about verbs, study pages 38–42.

- The verbs in the text are underlined below:

Emballé
C'est mangé!

Bientôt, quand tu manges des frites dans la rue, tu vas aussi manger l'emballage! Un Australien a inventé un cornet de frites en pomme de terre qui se mange comme un cornet de glace.
Les emballages qui traînent par terre – c'est fini.

- Which of these should you look up?
  - **inventé** is easy to guess.
  - You should know **vas** – it is part of the verb **aller** (to go). You should also know **est** – it is part of the verb **être** (to be). (See page 39.)
  - In the text there are three parts of the same verb: **manges, manger, mange**. You must know that if you look up your dictionary, you will find that all verbs are listed in the infinitive. (For more information about the infinitive, study page 38.) So you will find **manger** (to eat) listed in the dictionary, but not **manges** or **mange**. Similarly, you will find **traîner**, not **traînent**. **Traîner** is a verb with many meanings. Here it means 'to lie around'.

Answers

Exercise 5

1. • a small African boy
   • a lion
2. Either: they get separated
   or: they have a great adventure.
3. the director

Exercise 6

1. • pancakes (crêpes)
   • ice cream
2. by lift
3. end of March to end of September
4. 10 o'clock in the morning until 11 o'clock at night

Exercise 7

1. They are setting off on a world tour.
2. Any two of the following:
   • he wants to travel;
   • it's good for learning languages;
   • seeing how other people live in other countries.

Exercise 8

• Choose a quiet place.
• Try to find an animal or a bird which does not have too many other animals around it.

Exercise 9

1. The twins stretch out in front of the fire. Their mother tells them one of her stories.
2. A madman might kidnap her daughters or try to harm them.
3. Any three of the following:
   • she was the oldest of 5 children;
   • the family was poor;
   • her father was very strict;
   • weekends with the family were depressing.
4. She was put in a class where the level was too advanced for her.
5. to spend as much time as possible with her daughters
6. **(a)** writing for children
   (b) She has published 3 books for children and cassettes for the very young.

Exercise 10

1. an edible cone for chips (made of potato)
2. no wrappings lying around

4. Listening

When listening to French, don't expect to understand everything you hear. You don't need to!
Before you hear any French at all, you will be asked a question in English.
This means you will know what to concentrate on when listening – pick out only what you need to answer the question.

Key question words

Here are the key question words you will be asked in your Listening exam:

Now listen to **section three** on the tape. Work through the exercises in this section which help you concentrate on each key question word in turn.

Where?

Exercise 11

Listen to the five sentences in French on the tape which ask you to concentrate on **places** and answer these questions:

1. Where does this person live?
2. Where does this person do homework?
3. Where will you meet?
4. Where did this person spend two weeks?
5. Where would this person like to work?

When?

Exercise 12

This time, concentrate on **times** and **dates**.

1. When (what time) do lessons finish?
2. When are you invited to the cinema?
3. When did this person go to Greece?
4. When is the person leaving?
5. When (what date) is this person's birthday?

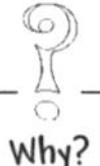

Why?

Exercise 13

Now listen for **reasons**.

1. Why can't this person come to school?
2. Why doesn't this person like chemistry?
3. Why does this person hate Camembert cheese?
4. Why can't this person come to the party on Saturday?
5. Why is this person going to Bordeaux?

Who?

Exercise 14

Now concentrate on **people**.

1. Who is this person introducing?
2. With whom did this person go on holiday?
3. With whom is this person going 'clubbing'?
4. Who is in the photograph?
5. Who will visit London next week?

How?

Exercise 15

This time, listen for '**how**'.

1. How does this person come to school?
2. How did this person cross the Channel?
3. How can you reserve your seat?
4. How does this person wish to pay?
5. How do you get in?

Exercise 16

Now listen for '**what**'.

1. What did this person get from her parents?
2. What two things does this person have in her bedroom?
3. What does this person do after school?
4. What is opposite the supermarket?
5. What does this person have for breakfast?

How many?

Exercise 17

Finally, listen for '**how many**'.

1. How many brothers and sisters does this person have?
2. How many pupils are there in this person's school?
3. How many bedrooms are there in this person's house?
4. How many apples did this person buy?
5. How many tropical fish does this person's uncle have?

Check your answers by looking at pages 24 and 25.

The importance of vocabulary

The best way of preparing for the Listening exam is to **learn** as much **vocabulary** as you can.

Remember **you do not have a dictionary for the Listening exam**, so the more words you know, the more likely you are to be able to make sense of what you hear.

- During your course, you can learn:
  - vocabulary lists in a textbook
  - vocabulary you have copied into a notebook
  - printed vocabulary lists your teacher has given you
  - or a combination of all of these.
- As you progress through your Standard Grade course and do your revision, you may find it useful to arrange your vocabulary under the following headings:
  - Self and Family
  - House and home
  - School
  - Leisure
  - Pets
  - Clothes
  - Food and Drink
  - Describing People
  - Times/Dates/Numbers
  - Holidays
  - Travel
  - Work and Money
  - Shopping
  - Feelings
  - Places and Facilities
  - Weather
  - Daily Routine

  If you know all your vocabulary under these headings, you will be well-prepared for the **Foundation** and **General** Listening exams.

- However, if you are aiming for **Credit**, you need to know **more**! Credit Listening exams in recent years have included items of public interest and current affairs in the French-speaking world.

  - For example, in a recent Credit Listening exam, the tape was about three student nurses who had just completed three weeks of practical training in Burkina Faso in Africa.
  Look at this list of some of the vocabulary which came up in that exam:

un étudiant	a student
faire un stage	to do a course
la plupart	most
les habitants	inhabitants
les malades	patients
tout	everything
un service hôtelier	meals provided
les médicaments	medicine
soigner	to look after

donner des cours	to give lessons
nourrir	to feed
équilibré	balanced
utiliser	to use/utilise
des produits	products
inutilisable	unusable
trois heures de marche three hours' walk	
c'était trop	it was too much
surnommé	nicknamed
fabriquer	to make
des jouets	toys
la formation	training
diagnostiquer	to diagnose
Le Tiers Monde	the Third World
un pays en voie de développement a developing country	
faire des études	to study

◦ But don't panic!

- Many of the words and phrases which come up in the Credit exam, and which are the key to getting the right answer, are very similar to English, but with French pronunciation!
- It would be a good idea to obtain a copy of Standard Grade French Past Papers so you can study the transcript of previous Credit Listening exams and increase your vocabulary.
- You should also start noting this type of current affairs vocabulary when you come across it in your reading.

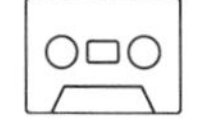

Now try exercise 18. Listen to the recording of 16 words and phrases in **section three** of the tape. They came up in a recent Credit Level exam.

Exercise 18

Write down the English meaning of the 16 words and phrases on the tape. Remember the tape was about nursing in hospitals in Africa.

Check your answers by looking at the answers and the transcript on pages 25 and 26.

- **Faux Amis**

are words which can catch you out. They do not mean in French what they sound like or look like in English! That is why they are called **faux amis** – 'false friends'.

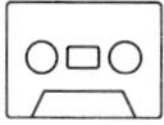

Listen to this list in **section three** of the tape. Learn these **faux amis** and make sure you're not caught out:

ancien	former
calme	quiet
chips	crisps
ennuyeux	boring
huit jours	a week
quinze jours	a fortnight
la journée	day
mille	thousand
rester	to stay
travailler	to work
la ville	town
les vacances	holidays
la cave	cellar
je me lave	I have a wash
le car	coach
l'hôtel de ville	town hall

Throughout your course, work on the following exercise.

Exercise 19

Add to this list if you find any more **faux amis** during your course.

The importance of numbers

Numbers in French are not easy and you can be sure that there will nearly always be numbers in any Listening exam.
The notes and exercises below will help you improve your ability to understand French numbers.

• Numbers 1–20

The numbers circled together below sound similar and are often confused.

Listen to **section four** of the tape and hear how each one is pronounced:

- 2 – **deux** 10 – **dix** 12 – **douze**
- 3 – **trois** 13 – **treize**
- 4 – **quatre** 14 – **quatorze**
- 5 – **cinq** 15 – **quinze**
- 6 – **six** 16 – **seize**

• Numbers 20–60

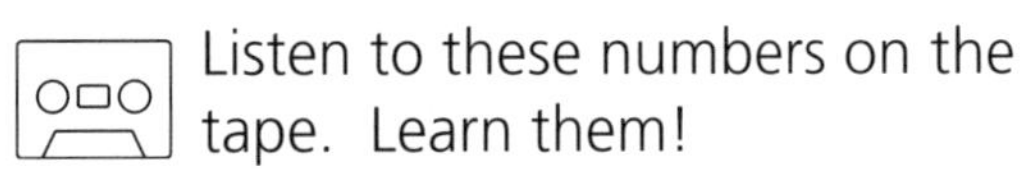

Listen to these numbers on the tape. Learn them!

20 – **vingt**
30 – **trente**
40 – **quarante**
50 – **cinquante**
60 – **soixante**

• Numbers 60–100

This is where French numbers are most tricky. Between 60 and 100, the French stop counting in tens and start counting in twenties. So, the word for 70 is 'sixty-ten' i.e. **soixante-dix**. 80 is 'four twenties' i.e. **quatre-vingts** and 90 is 'four twenties-ten' i.e. **quatre-vingt-dix**.

Listen to the numbers 60–100 on the tape.

- When listening to numbers 60–100, you have to be careful. Up to 60, you can simply write down the numbers as you hear them. For example, when you hear **quarante-cinq**, you know **quarante** is 40 and **cinq** is 5, so you write down **45**.
- However, after 60 it's different.
  - If you hear a number starting with **soixante-**, remember that the number could be 60-something **or** 70-something.
    For example, when you hear **soixante-seize**, you have to wait until you hear **seize**, which is 16, before you decide the number is **76**.
  - Similarly, if you hear a number starting with **quatre-vingt-**, this could be 80-something **or** 90-something.

Now try exercises 20 to 22 on the tape.

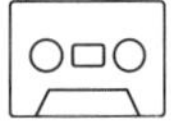

Listen to the numbers in French.

Exercise 20 (Numbers 1 – 20)

Write down the numbers (in figures) as you hear them.

Exercise 21 (Numbers 20 – 60)

Write down the numbers (in figures) as you hear them.

Exercise 22 (Numbers 60 – 100)

Write down the numbers (in figures) as you hear them.

Check your answers by looking at page 26.

- **Numbers 100+**
  - You must also know these higher numbers:
    100 – **cent**
    1000 – **mille**
    1 000 000 – **million**
  - Note these numbers above 100:
    105 – **cent cinq**
    500 – **cinq cents**
    504 – **cinq cent quatre**

- **Number phrases**
  - Here are a few phrases commonly used with numbers which you should know:

plus de	more than/over
moins de	less than/under
à peu près/ environ/vers	about/around/ approximately
une vingtaine	about 20
presque	almost

    les années quatre-vingts – the 80s
    dix-neuf cent quatre-vingt-seize – 1996
  - Watch the pronunciation of:
    six – 6 **huit** – 8 **dix** – 10
    When these appear in a phrase, the last letter is not sounded, e.g. **six pommes.**

Now try exercise 23 on the tape to practise your number phrases.

Listen to the tape. (The answers and the transcripts are on page 26.)

Exercise 23

1. When was this person born?
2. How many pears are in the basket?
3. How many people were at the party?
4. What is the population of this town?
5. Who gets in free?
6. When were fashions extraordinary?
7. How many brothers does he have?
8. How many dolls in this person's collection?
9. And in this person's?
10. How long will this person spend in the USA?

- One last hint for listening to numbers in French: when you hear a number, don't panic if you don't understand it immediately. Write it down – correct spelling is not important – or keep repeating it until you have time to think what it is in English.

Final hints

Finally, a few hints for effective Listening in the Standard Grade exam:

- At the start of the tape you will be introduced to the 'scenario' – this is the situation in which you will hear all the French. For example, you may have to imagine that:
  - a French pen-pal has sent you a tape, or
  - you are in France staying with a French pen-pal, or
  - you are on holiday in France with your family.

  Always bear the scenario in mind when writing your answers.
- Note how many marks are awarded for each question and try to find the same number of points as you listen. Don't write too much.
- Pay attention to the questions you are asked and listen out for key words and phrases.
- Concentrate 100% when the tape is playing. Remember you hear everything twice.
- The best time to make notes is between the first and second playing of each item. Don't write too much when the tape is playing – you may miss a key point.
- Remember the key word or phrase is often very like the English, but with a French pronunciation.
- Do not leave any blanks – you are guaranteed to get no marks if you do. Make a sensible guess if you have to.

Answers, transcripts and follow-up exercises

Exercise 11

Answers

1. Belgium
2. in her bedroom
3. outside the town hall
4. in the south of Spain
5. USA

Transcript

Now read the transcript of what you heard – the key phrase has been underlined.

1. J'habite en Belgique.
2. Je fais mes devoirs dans ma chambre.
3. Je te rencontre devant la mairie.
4. J'ai passé deux semaines dans le sud de l'Espagne.
5. Je voudrais travailler aux États-Unis.

Follow-up exercise

Now replace the key phrase with another possible answer of your own e.g.

1. J'habite en France.
2. Je fais mes devoirs ...
3. Je te rencontre ...
4. J'ai passé deux semaines ...
5. Je voudrais travailler ...

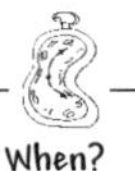

Exercise 12

Answers

1. 5 o'clock
2. Saturday evening
3. last year
4. today
5. 10th August

Transcript

The key phrase has been underlined.

1. Les cours finissent à cinq heures.
2. Tu veux aller au cinéma samedi soir?
3. L'année dernière je suis allée en Grèce.
4. Je pars aujourd'hui.
5. Mon anniversaire, c'est le 10 août.

Exercise 12 (cont.)

Follow-up exercise

Now replace the key phrase with another possible answer of your own e.g.

1. Les cours finissent à quatre heures et demie.
2. Tu veux aller au cinéma ...
3. ... je suis allé(e) en Grèce.
4. Je pars ...
5. Mon anniversaire, c'est ...

Exercise 13

Answers

1. She's not feeling well.
2. It's too difficult.
3. She finds it disgusting.
4. She's going away for the weekend.
5. to visit her aunt

Transcript

The key phrase has been underlined.

1. Je ne vais pas à l'école aujourd'hui – je me sens malade.
2. Je n'aime pas la chimie – c'est trop difficile.
3. Je déteste le Camembert – c'est dégoûtant.
4. Je ne peux pas venir à la boum samedi soir – je pars pour le weekend.
5. Je vais à Bordeaux pour rendre visite à ma tante.

Follow-up exercise

Now replace the key phrase with another possible answer of your own.

Exercise 14

Answers

1. her son
2. her parents
3. her friends
4. the woman's husband
5. President Chirac

Exercise 14 (cont.)

Transcript

The key phrase has been underlined.

1. Je te présente mon fils.
2. Je suis partie en vacances avec mes parents.
3. Demain soir je vais en boîte avec mes copains.
4. Voici une photo de mon mari.
5. Le Président Chirac va visiter Londres la semaine prochaine.

Follow-up exercise

Now replace the key phrase with another possible answer of your own.

Exercise 15

Answers

1. on foot
2. by hovercraft
3. phone the cinema
4. by credit card
5. ring the doorbell

Transcript

The key phrase has been underlined.

1. Je vais à l'école à pied.
2. J'ai traversé la Manche en aéroglisseur.
3. Pour réserver votre place, téléphonez au cinéma.
4. Je voudrais payer par carte de crédit.
5. Pour entrer, sonnez à la porte.

Exercise 16

Answers

1. a watch
2. a chest of drawers and a wardrobe
3. plays football
4. the post office
5. cereal

Transcript

The key phrase has been underlined.

1. J'ai reçu une montre de mes parents.
2. Dans ma chambre j'ai une commode et une armoire.
3. Après l'école je joue au foot.
4. La poste est en face du supermarché.
5. Pour le petit déjeuner je prends des céréales.

Exercise 16 (cont.)

Follow-up exercise

Now replace the key phrase with another possible answer of your own.

Exercise 17

Answers

1. 1 sister and 2 brothers
2. 850
3. 3
4. 6
5. lots

Transcript

The key phrase has been underlined.

1. J'ai une soeur et deux frères.
2. Il y a huit cent cinquante élèves à mon école.
3. Chez nous, on a trois chambres.
4. J'ai acheté six pommes pour notre pique-nique.
5. Mon oncle a beaucoup de poissons tropicaux.

Exercise 18

Answers

1. practical
2. territory
3. an independent republic
4. agriculture
5. to pay
6. finance their operation
7. abandoned by their family
8. paediatrics
9. dehydrated
10. suffered from malnutrition or malaria
11. use the products of the region
12. Chinese incubators
13. The instructions are written in Chinese.
14. less technical and more practical
15. obtained our diploma
16. organise a permanent exchange

Exercise 18 (cont.)

Transcript

1. pratique
2. territoire
3. une république indépendante
4. l'agriculture
5. payer
6. financer leur opération
7. abandonnés par leur famille
8. pédiatrie
9. déshydratés
10. souffraient de malnutrition ou de malaria
11. utilisent les produits de la région
12. incubateurs chinois
13. Les instructions sont écrites en chinois.
14. moins technique et plus pratique
15. obtenu notre diplôme
16. organiser un échange permanent

Exercise 20 (Numbers 1 – 20)

	Answers	Transcript
1.	3	trois
2.	16	seize
3.	4	quatre
4.	15	quinze
5.	12	douze
6.	2	deux
7.	14	quatorze
8.	10	dix
9.	5	cinq
10.	13	treize

Exercise 21 (Numbers 20 – 60)

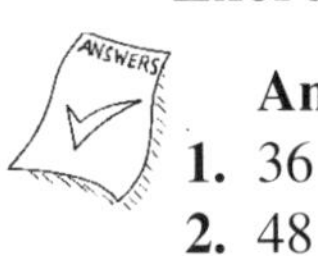

	Answers	Transcript
1.	36	trente-six
2.	48	quarante-huit
3.	27	vingt-sept
4.	51	cinquante et un
5.	42	quarante-deux
6.	39	trente-neuf
7.	25	vingt-cinq
8.	43	quarante-trois
9.	50	cinquante
10.	34	trente-quatre

Exercise 22 (Numbers 60 – 100)

	Answers	Transcript
1.	63	soixante-trois
2.	73	soixante-treize
3.	89	quatre-vingt-neuf
4.	74	soixante-quatorze
5.	87	quatre-vingt-sept
6.	96	quatre-vingt-seize
7.	64	soixante-quatre
8.	95	quatre-vingt-quinze
9.	78	soixante-dix-huit
10.	92	quatre-vingt-douze

Exercise 23

Answers

1. 1979
2. 8
3. about 30
4. about 10 000
5. under 12s
6. in the 70s
7. 6
8. almost 100
9. more than 150
10. about 3 months

Transcript

The key phrase has been underlined.

1. Je suis née en dix-neuf cent soixante-dix-neuf.
2. J'ai huit poires dans mon panier.
3. Il y avait une trentaine de personnes à la boum hier soir.
4. Cette ville a dix mille habitants à peu près.
5. L'entrée est gratuite pour les enfants de moins de douze ans.
6. Pendant les années soixante-dix on portait des vêtements extraordinaires.
7. Imagine! Il a six frères!
8. J'ai presque cent poupées dans ma collection.
9. Et alors? Moi, j'en ai plus de cent cinquante!
10. Je vais passer trois mois environ aux États-Unis.

5. Writing at General Level

Do not imagine that writing in French is too difficult for you. To be successful you need to follow the hints below and you need a lot of practice to give you confidence in your own ability.

General Level hints

Follow these hints to be successful in the General Level Writing exam:

- Read the question(s) closely and consider the topic carefully.
- Answer the question(s)! Ensure you have included all the details requested.
- Aim to write **three simple sentences** but remember this may not be enough in every case.
  - Try to think of what you know in French. Do not think in English and then translate.
  - Write only what is easy and familiar to you.
  - Keep the vocabulary simple.
  - Do not overuse your dictionary.
  - Remember what you learnt for Speaking – you can transfer what you learnt there to Writing.
- From the start of your Standard Grade course, learn basic grammar:
  - You are usually required to write about things that happened in the past in at least one section of the exam. Study section 4 on page 29, and the notes on the perfect tense on page 40.
  - You are often required to ask questions in at least one section of the exam. Study section 3 on page 29 and the notes on Asking Questions on pages 44–47.

Writing about yourself

Be prepared to write three simple sentences on each of the topics below. Here are three possible sentences for each topic:

Personal details
- Je m'appelle Sarah Williams.
- J'ai 15 ans.
- J'habite à Leslie.

School
- Mon collège s'appelle Woodvale.
- Il y a 8 cours par jour.
- J'étudie le français.

A holiday
- L'année dernière je suis allé(e) en Italie.
- J'ai fait de la natation.
- Il a fait très chaud.

Personal description
- Je suis mince.
- J'ai les cheveux mi-longs.
- J'ai les yeux noisette.

Family
- J'habite avec mes parents à Glenrothes.
- J'ai un frère.
- Il s'appelle Michael.

Pets
- J'adore les animaux.
- J'ai un chien à la maison.
- Il s'appelle Rover.

Leisure Interests
- Quand je suis libre le soir, je regarde la télé.
- Le samedi après-midi, je vais en ville.
- Mon sport préféré, c'est l'équitation.

Television
- Je regarde la télé tous les soirs.
- J'aime les feuilletons et les émissions de musique.
- Je déteste les informations – c'est barbant.

Money
- Je reçois dix livres par semaine.
- D'habitude j'achète des bonbons et des magazines.
- Je fais des économies pour mes vacances.

House
- J'habite une maison jumelée à Cowdenbeath.
- Chez moi, il y a trois chambres.
- En plus j'ai un grand jardin.

Home-town or area
- J'habite à Kelty, un village dans l'est de l'Écosse.
- À Kelty, il y a des magasins et une MJC.
- Il n'y a pas de cinéma.

Food and Drink
- Pour le petit déjeuner, je prends des tartines.
- Je prends le déjeuner à la cantine du collège.
- J'aime le poulet et les frites.

Daily Routine
- Je me lève à sept heures.
- Les cours commencent à neuf heures.
- Je rentre à la maison à quatre heures.

Work
- Je livre des journaux le matin.
- Je gagne douze livres par semaine.
- Après avoir quitté l'école, je voudrais être vétérinaire.

To help you develop your Listening and Speaking skills, listen to all of these sentences on **section five** of the tape. Repeat each sentence aloud as you hear it.

Now try exercise 24.

Exercise 24

The sentences above that you have just read and heard on the tape do not, of course, match your own personal details! So, rewrite all the sentences above, changing the details to suit your own circumstances.

General Level Writing Paper example

Here is an example of a General Level Writing Paper. See how important it is to be able to write about yourself.

Pay attention to the following points:

- all required details are given
- answers are minimal, however
- it's straightforward, but correct!

You are writing to your French pen-pal for the first time.

1. Give some details about yourself. You may wish to include your name, age and information about your family, e.g.

   Je m'appelle Paul/Shona.
   J'ai 15 ans.
   J'ai une soeur. Elle s'appelle Emma.
   J'ai un chat.

2. Write about your school now. You can include its name, when school starts and finishes, your favourite and least favourite subjects, e.g.

   Mon collège s'appelle Woodvale High.
   Les cours commencent à 9 heures.
   J'aime l'anglais et je déteste les maths.

3. Ask some questions about your pen-pal's house. You may want to find out about its size, how many rooms it has, if there is a garden, e.g.

   Est-ce que ta maison est grande ou petite?
   Il y a un jardin?
   Il y a combien de pièces?

4. You've already been to France – last year you were on holiday in Paris. Tell your pen-pal what you saw, where you stayed, e.g.

   Je suis allé(e) à Paris avec ma mère.
   J'ai logé dans un hôtel.
   J'ai vu la Tour Eiffel et l'Arc de Triomphe.

5. You have no recent photo of yourself so write a description of yourself. You might include your height, hair and eye colour, e.g.

   Je suis petit(e).
   J'ai les cheveux blonds et courts.
   J'ai les yeux bleus.

Now try exercise 25.

Exercise 25

Write your own answers to the five sections above.

Writing notes

Quite often in the General Writing Paper, you are asked to write a note in French.

Try exercises 26 and 27, studying the hints to help you:

Exercise 26

You are staying with your French pen-pal's family. The phone rings when you are alone in the house and you have to write a message for someone.

- Remember you should aim to write **three simple sentences**. In this case they could be:
  - who phoned
  - a message
  - a reason or instruction.

- Now look at the vocabulary you could use:

◦ **who phoned?**

Marie		
Ta Your	**mère** mother **grand-mère** grandmother **tante** aunt **copine** friend (female)	**a téléphoné.** telephoned.
Ton Your	**père** father **grand-père** grandfather **oncle** uncle **copain** friend (male)	
Votre Your	**mari** husband **femme** wife	

◦ **message**

Il/Elle He/She	**va être en retard** will be late **ne vient pas** is not coming **arrive** is arriving	**samedi.** on Saturday. **ce soir.** this evening. **cet après-midi.** this afternoon. **aujourd'hui.** today. **demain.** tomorrow. **à sept heures.** at 7 o'clock.
Il/Elle He/She	**t'invite** is inviting you	**à sa boum.** to his/her party. **au cinéma.** to the cinema.

◦ **reason**

- **Il/Elle est malade.** He/she is ill.
- **Sa voiture est en panne.** His/her car has broken down.

◦ **instruction**

Va **Allez**	**le** **la**	**chercher**	**à la gare.** **à l'aéroport.**
Pick	him her	up	at the station. at the airport.

Attends **Attendez** Expect	**-le** him **-la** her	**vers huit heures.** around 8 o'clock.

- **Prépare un bon dîner!** Get a good dinner ready!
- **Ça commence vers sept heures et demie.** It starts about 7.30.
- **Rendez-vous à sept heures.** Meet at 7 o'clock.

Exercise 27

While staying with your pen-pal, you have to go out and leave a note to say where you have gone.

- In this case your three sentences could be:
  - where you have gone
  - why
  - what time you'll be back.

- Here's some French you could use:
  - **where you have gone**

Je suis allé(e) I have gone	**en ville.** into town. **chez Jean-Paul.** round to Jean-Paul's. **au centre sportif.** to the sports centre. **au supermarché.** to the supermarket.

- **why**

Je veux I want	**faire du shopping** to do some shopping **acheter des chips** to buy some crisps **acheter des souvenirs** to buy some souvenirs **écouter de la musique** to listen to music **jouer au badminton** to play badminton
pour in order	

- **what time you'll be back**

Je rentre } **vers sept heures.**
Je reviens }

I'll be home } about 7 o'clock.
I'll be back }

Now try exercises 28 to 32 using some of the words and phrases on this page and page 30.

Exercise 28

Write a note in French telling your pen-pal that his grandmother will be late this evening and to expect her around 8 o'clock.

Exercise 29

Write a note in French telling your pen-pal that his friend Didier phoned, inviting him to a party on Saturday, starting about 9 o'clock.

Exercise 30

Write a note in French telling your pen-pal's mother that her husband phoned to say he's arriving at 7.30 this evening and to meet him at the airport.

Exercise 31

Write a note in French telling your pen-pal that you've gone into town to do some shopping and that you'll be home around 4 o'clock.

Exercise 32

Write a note in French telling your pen-pal that you've gone round to Sandrine's house to listen to music and you'll be back at midday.

Remember to start your notes off with **Cher** ... (to a boy) or **Chère** ... (to a girl) and to sign your name at the end.

You'll find possible answers to exercises 28 to 32 on page 32.

Writing postcards

- Three simple sentences on a postcard could be about:
  - where you are
  - what the weather is like
  - what you're doing or have been doing, or a general comment.
- For example, here's a postcard from someone on holiday in the French Alps:

Salut Anne! Me voici dans les Alpes! Je fais du ski tous les jours. C'est magnifique! Amitiés, Pamela	Mlle Anne Dupont 46 Rue de la Source 33000 Bordeaux

and another one from St Tropez:

Salut Paul! Me voici à St Tropez! Hier, j'ai fait de la planche à voile. Il fait un temps superbe. Amitiés, Chris	M. Paul St Val 16 Rue de Versailles 75000 Paris

Now try exercises 33 to 35.
(Possible answers are below.)

Exercise 33

Write a postcard from Paris where you visited the Louvre yesterday. You think Paris is a great city.

Exercise 34

Write a postcard from Strasbourg where you're on holiday with your sister. The weather is fine and you have visited the cathedral.

Exercise 35

Write a postcard from Annecy where the scenery is fabulous and you've been swimming in the lake.

Answers

Exercise 28

Cher Michel,
Ta grand-mère a téléphoné. Elle va être en retard ce soir. Attends-la vers huit heures.
Peter

Exercise 29

Cher Thierry,
Ton copain, Didier, a téléphoné. Il t'invite à sa boum samedi. Ça commence vers neuf heures.
Kelly

Exercise 30

Chère Madame Chapelut,
Votre mari a téléphoné. Il arrive à sept heures et demie ce soir. Allez le chercher à l'aéroport.
Fiona

Exercise 31

Chère Delphine,
Je suis allée en ville. Je veux faire du shopping.
Je rentre vers quatre heures.
Sarah

Exercise 32

Chère Colette,
Je suis allé chez Sandrine pour écouter de la musique. Je reviens à midi.
À bientôt! Stephen

Exercise 33

Salut Geneviève!
Me voici à Paris. Hier j'ai visité le Louvre.
Quelle ville passionnante!
Amitiés, Gwen

Exercise 34

Salut Pascal!
Me voici à Strasbourg avec ma soeur. Hier on a visité la cathédrale. Il fait beau ici.
Amitiés, Stewart

Exercise 35

Salut Florian!
Me voici à Annecy. Le paysage est superbe!
Hier j'ai nagé dans le lac.
Amitiés, Colin

6. Writing at Credit Level

Credit Level hints

Study again the General Level hints on page 27, most of which are also important for Credit Level Writing. In addition, follow these extra hints for Credit Level Writing:

- Plan your essay. Remember to have an introduction and a conclusion.
- Be prepared to express opinions and feelings.
- Make your French grammatically accurate.
- Do not be tempted to reuse phrases word for word from the French paragraphs in the question paper.
- Do not write too much. Concentrate on quality. Do not exceed the word limit at Credit Level.
- Be confident – limit your use of your dictionary.
- Have a store of useful words and phrases at your fingertips.
- After you have finished your essay, check your work thoroughly and systematically. Check verbs, adjectives, gender, accents and spelling.

Useful words and phrases

Here are some useful words and phrases to get you started:

à mon avis	in my opinion
d'un côté ... de l'autre (côté)	on the one hand ... on the other hand
souvent	often
rarement	rarely
de temps en temps	now and again
une fois par { semaine / mois	once a { week / month
après avoir ...	after having ...
(e.g. **après avoir mangé**	after having eaten)
avant de ...	before ______ing ...
(e.g. **avant de partir**	before leaving)
en général	in general
d'habitude	usually
quelquefois	sometimes
parce que	because
puisque	since
je pense que ...	I think that ...
je crois que ...	I believe that ...
je trouve que ...	I think that ...
d'abord	first of all
ensuite	then/next
en plus	moreover
puis	then
enfin / **finalement**	finally
pour conclure	to conclude

To help you develop your Speaking skills as well as your Writing skills, listen to all these useful words and phrases read aloud in **section six** on the tape. Repeat them aloud as you hear each one.

Holiday essay example

Here is an example of a Credit Level essay to show what you could write for the following topic:

Write approximately 200 words on the topic of holidays, including what you like and don't like to do on holiday and an account of a holiday you have had in the past.

Moi, j'adore les vacances, surtout les grandes vacances quand on a sept semaines de libre. Pas de profs, ni de devoirs pendant deux mois!

D'habitude, je pars pendant deux semaines avec ma famille. On choisit toujours un pays où il fait chaud et où il y a beaucoup à faire pour tout le monde. Mes parents aiment visiter des monuments et des sites historiques, tandis que moi, je déteste ça. Je préfère rester à la plage, me bronzer et faire de la natation. Ma soeur, au contraire, est très sportive. Elle aime faire de la planche à voile, du ski nautique et de la plongée sous-marine. Quelles vacances fatigantes!

L'année dernière, je suis allé(e) en Grèce. J'ai passé une quinzaine de jours sur l'île de Rhodes. J'ai voyagé en avion de Glasgow à Rhodes. J'ai logé dans un hôtel où il y avait une piscine et un très bon restaurant.

Chaque jour, j'ai nagé, j'ai fait des bains de soleil. En plus, j'ai fait des excursions sur l'île. J'ai visité la vieille ville de Rhodes où on peut faire un tour des murs et faire les magasins touristiques. J'ai vu aussi la vallée des papillons.

Le soir, j'ai mangé dans un restaurant et quelquefois je suis allé(e) en boîte. Quel séjour superbe!

Pour conclure, je crois que les vacances sont très importantes. On a l'occasion de voyager un peu et de voir d'autres pays et de se relaxer avec la famille ou des copains.

Notice that:

- the essay has an introduction and a conclusion
- it is written in paragraphs which relate to the different parts of the question
- it uses several of the useful words and phrases on page 33
- it expresses opinions and feelings.

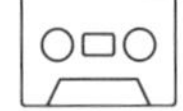

To help you develop your Listening and Reading skills as well as your Writing skills, listen to this essay read aloud in **section seven** of the tape. After listening, see if you can write a short summary in English of the main points of the essay.

School essay

Try the following exercise. Study the hints to help you.

> **Exercise 36**
>
> Write an essay on 'l'école', answering these questions:
>
> **1.** What is a typical school day for you?
> **2.** What subjects do you do?
> **3.** Do you have much homework?
> **4.** What do you think of school in general?
> **5.** What are you going to do after you leave school?

- It is vital that you first **plan** your essay – you will get some ideas of how to do this by using the questions in the exam paper. If you answer these questions, you have the bulk of your essay. Remember to have an introduction and a conclusion, no matter how short they might be. Here is a possible plan for your essay on school, in the form of a **list**, with useful phrases underneath:

◦ **Introduction**
- Mon collège s'appelle ...
- Il est assez grand.

◦ **School day**
- Je vais au collège en autobus.
- J'arrive au collège à ...
- Les cours commencent à ... et finissent à ...
- la récréation?
- Pendant la récréation ...
- Pendant l'heure du déjeuner ...

◦ **Subjects**

– Likes/Dislikes	**– Reasons**
· J'adore ...	· C'est amusant.
· J'aime ...	· Le prof est stricte.
· Je n'aime pas ...	· Je suis { fort(e) en ...
· Je préfère ...	{ faible en ...

◦ **School**

– Good points
- L'école, c'est important pour la vie future.
- J'aime voir mes copains tous les jours.

– Bad Points
- Les examens sont difficiles.
- On a trop de devoirs.
- C'est ennuyeux, quelquefois.

◦ **After leaving school**
- Je vais travailler ... }
- Je voudrais travailler comme ... } parce que ...

◦ **Conclusion**
- À mon avis l'école, c'est ...

- Next, as you write your essay, tick off each section of the plan as you complete that paragraph. If you follow this approach, your essay will read well, be organised and save you time in the long run. Also, you will not be in danger of repeating yourself.
- You can, however, rearrange your answers, add extras, concentrate on only a couple of areas and try to 'show off' your French, aiming to write approximately 200 words, the length of essay which is required at Credit Level.
- Remember to consider the tenses you will use.
- It is also worthwhile noting down a selection of useful words and phrases to include, so you do not forget all about them.

Home-town essay

Try the following exercise. Study the hints to help you.

Exercise 37

Write approximately 200 words on the topic of your home-town and whether you like it there or would prefer to live somewhere else.

- First, make a **plan**. The **spider graph** below is an alternative way of planning your essay (rather than making a list as in exercises 36 and 38).

Home-town

- **Say where it is.**
  - Kirkcaldy, c'est une ville qui se trouve dans l'est de l'Écosse dans la région de Fife.
- **Say what there is there.**
  - Il y a ...
  - Il y a beaucoup de ...
  - Il y a pas mal de ...
- **Say what there isn't there.**
  - Il n'y a pas de ...
  - Il y a peu de ...
  - Il n'y a pas assez de ...
- **Say whether you like living there. Give reasons.**
  - J'aime habiter à Kirkcaldy.
  - J'ai beaucoup de copains qui y habitent.
- **Say what you don't like about it.**
  - Il y a trop de circulation et de bruit.
  - Il n'y a pas grand-chose à faire.
- **Say where you'd prefer to live. Describe your ideal town.**
  - Moi, je voudrais habiter à ...
  - C'est une grande ville où il y a beaucoup de choses à faire ...
  - Ma ville idéale se trouve aux États-Unis près de Miami.

- Next, make sure you also cover the other hints to exercise 36.

Leisure essay

Try the following exercise. Study the hints to help you.

Exercise 38

Write about your leisure time – what you do, when, where and with whom. Say why you think it's important to have leisure time.

• First, make a **plan**. This time write a **list** to help plan your essay.
Use the questions as paragraph headings. List them, and any relevant ideas of your own, on your answer page. Don't forget to include an introduction and a conclusion and to give your opinions. Your list might look like this, with your ideas noted under each heading:

- **Introduction**
  - J'ai beaucoup de passe-temps.
  - Je sors.
  - Je reste à la maison.
- **What I do**
  - Je fais mes devoirs.
  - Je regarde la télé.
  - J'écoute de la musique.
  - Je vais en ville.
  - Je fais du shopping.
  - Je rencontre mes amis.
- **When**
  - après les cours
  - le soir
  - pendant le weekend
  - quand il fait { beau / mauvais
- **Where**
  - chez moi
  - au centre sportif
  - à la piscine
  - chez des copains
  - en ville
  - à la discothèque
- **With whom**
  - avec mes copains
  - avec ma famille
  - tout(e) seul(e)
- **Conclusion** (importance of leisure)
  - Pendant mes heures de loisirs j'aime:
    – me décontracter
    – oublier le collège
    – faire du sport
    – rencontrer des amis.
  - Il est important de ne pas travailler tout le temps.

• Next, make sure you also cover the other hints to exercise 36.

Now, having studied this chapter carefully, try exercise 39:

Exercise 39

Plan and write an essay about your free time, answering these questions:

1. What are your favourite pastimes?
2. Do you spend a lot of money on them?
3. Do you mostly spend your free time at home or do you prefer to go out?
4. Do you prefer to be with friends or do you like to spend time alone?

7. Grammar

Grammar is the study of how words are put together to make sentences.
It is important for every skill: Speaking, Reading, Listening and Writing.
Learning grammar helps you to understand more accurately what you read and hear. It helps you to speak well and write accurately.

It is impossible to cover all the areas of Grammar in these *Notes*. However, you will find the main areas are covered. First, study again page 17 which introduces some areas of grammar. Now let's concentrate on these areas:

- Nouns
- Verbs
- Adjectives
- Asking questions
- Impressive phrases

Nouns

As noted on page 17, a noun is the name of a person or a thing, e.g. 'cat', 'Joanne', 'photocopier' and 'beauty'.

All nouns in French are either masculine or feminine. This is called their gender.

- The word for 'the' in French is:
  - **le** before a masculine singular noun
  - **la** before a feminine singular noun
  - **l'** before a noun beginning with a vowel
  - **les** before any plural noun.
- The word for 'a' in French is:
  - **un** before a masculine singular noun
  - **une** before a feminine singular noun.
- The word for 'some' in French is:
  - **du** before a masculine singular noun
  - **de la** before a feminine singular noun
  - **de l'** before any singular noun beginning with a vowel
  - **des** before all plural nouns.

Learn the gender of nouns in French when you are learning their meaning, e.g. **le nez** (nose), **la dent** (tooth), **l'eau** *nf* (water) and **l'âge** *nm* (age).

Most nouns in French add **-s** to become plural. However, there are exceptions, for example, some add **-x** to become plural.

Verbs

Verbs are 'doing' or 'being' words, for example 'give', 'go', 'work' and 'have'.
Verbs are listed in the dictionary in the infinitive form. In English, when a verb is in the infinitive, it has 'to' in front of it, e.g. 'to watch', 'to finish' and 'to sell'. In French, when a verb is in the infinitive, it ends in **-er**, **-ir** or **-re**, e.g. **regarder**, **finir** and **vendre**.
Verbs are very important: without a verb, you have no sentence!

- There are three **tenses** you should know:
  - the **present** tense
  - the **perfect** tense
  - the **immediate future** tense.
- In addition, there is a special type of verb called a **reflexive** verb.

Let's now concentrate on these three tenses and then reflexive verbs.

The Present Tense

is used to describe what is happening **now**, at the present moment.

- Learn these three **regular** forms of the present tense:

donner	to give	vendre	to sell	finir	to finish
je donne	I give	je vends	I sell	je finis	I finish
tu donnes	you give	tu vends	you sell	tu finis	you finish
il	he gives	il	he sells	il	he finishes
elle } donne	she gives	elle } vend	she sells	elle } finit	she finishes
on	we give	on	we sell	on	we finish
nous donnons	we give	nous vendons	we sell	nous finissons	we finish
vous donnez	you give	vous vendez	you sell	vous finissez	you finish
ils } donnent	they give	ils } vendent	they sell	ils } finissent	they finish
elles	they give	elles	they sell	elles	they finish

You will now be able to cope with most verbs in the present tense.

- There are also some **irregular** verbs – they do not fit into the regular forms above. Learn these four very important ones:

avoir	to have	être	to be	aller	to go	faire	to do
j'ai	I have	je suis	I am	je vais	I go	je fais	I do
tu as	you have	tu es	you are	tu vas	you go	tu fais	you do
il	he has	il	he is	il	he goes	il	he does
elle } a	she has	elle } est	she is	elle } va	she goes	elle } fait	she does
on	we have	on	we are	on	we go	on	we do
nous avons	we have	nous sommes	we are	nous allons	we go	nous faisons	we do
vous avez	you have	vous êtes	you are	vous allez	you go	vous faites	you do
ils } ont	they have	ils } sont	they are	ils } vont	they go	ils } font	they do
elles	they have	elles	they are	elles	they go	elles	they do

Some other important verbs are irregular too.

Try the following exercise.

Exercise 40

Write out the present tense of these other irregular verbs in full, using your dictionary for help:

vouloir	to want	**boire**	to drink	**voir**	to see	**connaître**	to know (a person)
pouvoir	to be able (can)	**lire**	to read	**venir**	to come	**écrire**	to write

- Finally, remember that you can translate the present tense in French in two ways, e.g.
  - **je donne** can be translated as 'I give' or 'I am giving'
  - **tu vends** can be translated as 'you sell' or 'you are selling'
  - **elle finit** can be translated as 'she finishes' or 'she is finishing'
  - **nous avons** can be translated as 'we have' or 'we are having'
  - **vous allez** can be translated as 'you go' or 'you are going'.

The Perfect Tense

is used to describe what happened in the **past**.

- To form the perfect tense of **regular** verbs:

◦ you need an **auxiliary** verb. Most verbs have **avoir** as their auxiliary verb. Here is a whole verb written out to show you how:

j'ai vendu	I sold/have sold
tu as vendu	you sold/have sold
il a vendu	he sold/has sold
elle a vendu	she sold/has sold
on a vendu	we sold/have sold
nous avons vendu	we sold/have sold
vous avez vendu	you sold/have sold
ils ont vendu	they sold/have sold
elles ont vendu	they sold/have sold

◦ you need to make a **past participle**:

- **-er** verbs change to end in **-é**
- **-ir** verbs change to end in **-i**
- **-re** verbs change to end in **-u**

Here are some examples:

- donner ⇒ donn<u>é</u>
- regarder ⇒ regard<u>é</u>
- choisir ⇒ chois<u>i</u>
- finir ⇒ fin<u>i</u>
- vendre ⇒ vend<u>u</u>
- attendre ⇒ attend<u>u</u>

- You will find yet again that some verbs are **irregular**, however. Here are four important ones:

◦ voir ⇒ j'ai vu ◦ boire ⇒ j'ai bu ◦ lire ⇒ j'ai lu ◦ écrire ⇒ j'ai écrit

Try exercise 41.

Exercise 41

Write out the perfect tense of these other irregular verbs in full, using your dictionary for help.

vouloir **rire** **avoir**
pouvoir **faire** **devoir**

- Some other verbs act a bit **differently**: they have **être** instead of **avoir** as their auxiliary verb. Here are two examples – **aller** and **partir**:

aller	to go	partir	to leave
je suis allé(e)	I went	je suis parti(e)	I left
tu es allé(e)	you went	tu es parti(e)	you left
il est allé	he went	il est parti	he left
elle est allée	she went	elle est partie	she left
on est allé(e)	we went	on est parti(e)	we left
nous sommes allés (allées)	we went	nous sommes partis (parties)	we left
vous êtes allé(e) (allés/allées)	you went	vous êtes parti(e) (partis/parties)	you left
ils sont allés	they went	ils sont partis	they left
elles sont allées	they went	elles sont parties	they left

Verbs which have **être** as their auxiliary verb add **-e** for feminine and **-s** for plural onto their past participle. The alternative endings tell whether the person or item is male or female, singular or plural.

Now try exercise 42.

Exercise 42

Can you find any other verbs which have **être** as their auxiliary verb?

The Immediate Future Tense

is used to describe what you're **going to do** in the future.
To form the immediate future tense, use the present tense of **aller**, plus another verb in the infinitive. (See page 38 for more about the infinitive.)

- Here are some examples:
  - Je vais travailler dans un supermarché. — I'm going to work in a supermarket.
  - Je vais choisir des cadeaux. — I'm going to choose some presents.
  - Je vais vendre mon vélo. — I'm going to sell my bicycle.

- You might be asked **questions** like the following:

- Qu'est-ce que tu vas faire ce soir? — What are you going to do tonight?

- Qu'est-ce que tu vas faire pendant les vacances? — What are you going to do during the holidays?

- Qu'est-ce que tu vas faire quand tu quitteras le collège? — What are you going to do when you leave school?

- Now consider some possible **answers**:

- Je vais rencontrer mes copains. — I'm going to meet my friends.
- Je vais finir mes devoirs. — I'm going to finish my homework.
- Je vais faire mes commissions. — I'm going to do my shopping.

- Je vais voyager en France. — I'm going to travel to France.
- Je vais partir en Suisse. — I'm going to go to Switzerland.
- Je vais descendre du train à Genève. — I'm going to get off the train at Geneva.

- Je vais trouver un emploi. — I'm going to find a job.
- Je vais rendre visite à mes cousins qui habitent à l'étranger. — I'm going to visit my cousins who live abroad.
- Je vais rougir. Je ne sais pas! — I'm going to blush. I don't know!

Try the following exercise.

Exercise 43

1. Write some more sentences in the immediate future tense, by starting with **Je vais ....**
2. Now change the sentences a little, so you alter their meanings. For example, start with **Il va ...** or **Elles vont ....** What do they mean now?
3. Finally, start all the sentences with **Tu vas ....** Add a question mark at the end and, when speaking, raise your voice at the end of the sentence. Now you've made up a lot of questions!

- Now not only have you learned how to make and use the immediate future tense, you've also learned how to make up simple questions.

Reflexive Verbs

are special: they describe actions you do to yourself. They are often used when you describe your daily routine. All reflexive verbs have **se** before the infinitive. **Se** means 'self' literally and changes according to who is doing the action. For example, here is the reflexive verb **se laver** (to wash oneself):

- in the **present tense**:

je me lave	I wash myself
tu te laves	you wash yourself
il se lave	he washes himself
elle se lave	she washes herself
on se lave	we wash ourselves
nous nous lavons	we wash ourselves
vous vous lavez	you wash yourself/yourselves
ils se lavent	they wash themselves
elles se lavent	they wash themselves

- in the **perfect tense**:

je me suis lavé(e)	I washed myself
tu t'es lavé(e)	you washed yourself
il s'est lavé	he washed himself
elle s'est lavée	she washed herself
on s'est lavé(e)	we washed ourselves
nous nous sommes lavés (lavées)	we washed ourselves
vous vous êtes lavé(e)/lavés (lavées)	you washed yourself/yourselves
ils se sont lavés	they washed themselves
elles se sont lavées	they washed themselves

Note that the auxiliary verb is **être** and that there are alternative endings.

Try the following exercise.

Exercise 44

1. Look up the following reflexives in your dictionary:
   se réveiller **se coucher** **se déshabiller**
   se lever **s'habiller** **se reposer**
2. Now write out the verbs in the present and perfect tenses.

Now you will see why daily routine is important.

Now go back to page 39 and listen to the French read aloud in **section eight** of the tape. Repeat each verb aloud as you hear it.

Adjectives

Adjectives are describing words, for example 'new', 'good', 'red' and 'tall'. They are important because they add a lot of meaning to a phrase or sentence.

- Adjectives in French sometimes **change** their **spelling** depending on what they're describing. What you must consider is the noun that they're describing – is the noun masculine or feminine, singular or plural?

  - Most adjectives add the letter **-e** for feminine singular, **-es** for feminine plural and **-s** for masculine plural. Here are some examples:

Masc	Plural	Fem	Plural	
grand	grands	grande	grandes	big
petit	petits	petite	petites	small
âgé	âgés	âgée	âgées	old
intelligent	intelligents	intelligente	intelligentes	intelligent

  - But here are some other adjectives which change quite a bit:

Masc	Plural	Fem	Plural	
blanc	blancs	blanche	blanches	white
mignon	mignons	mignonne	mignonnes	cute
beau	beaux	belle	belles	beautiful
frais	frais	fraîche	fraîches	fresh
vieux	vieux	vieille	vieilles	old
bon	bons	bonne	bonnes	good

  - Some other adjectives have very few alterations. Can you find the slight change in the following?

Masc	Plural	Fem	Plural	
riche	riches	riche	riches	rich
pauvre	pauvres	pauvre	pauvres	poor
jeune	jeunes	jeune	jeunes	young
moderne	modernes	moderne	modernes	old

- You must also consider the **position** of adjectives. Most adjectives sit **after** the noun they describe; some others sit **before**. Learn this list of adjectives that are placed before the noun. You will see that those which come before are all very commonly used.
  - Some of the adjectives which come **before** the noun are:

adjective noun

grand	big	**bon**	good
jeune	young	**mauvais**	bad
vieux	old	**beau**	handsome, beautiful
petit	small	**joli**	pretty
nouveau	new		

Throughout your Standard Grade course, work on the following exercise.

Exercise 45

Add to this list of adjectives which come **before** the noun.

◦ Finally, **colours**.
They sit **after** the noun they describe. Here are some examples:

un tricot noir	a black jumper
un sac jaune	a yellow bag
une souris blanche	a white mouse
une voiture verte	a green car
des crayons bleus	blue pencils
des chaussures blanches	white shoes

- Note down any unknown adjectives you come across and find out their meanings.
- Don't ignore adjectives when reading or listening. Be precise in your answer: include the adjective – it may be a key word and worth a mark.
- Use adjectives in your Writing:
  - at General Level if you're asked to describe somebody or something
  - at Credit Level to add detail and interest to your essay.

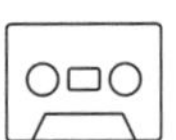
Now go back to page 43 and listen to the adjectives as they are read out in **section nine** of the tape. Repeat each adjective aloud as you hear it.

Asking questions

Being able to ask and answer questions is important in all parts of the course, but especially in General Level Writing where you are often asked to write questions.

- Learn these **key question words** and **phrases**:

Qui?	Who?
Quand?	When?
Depuis quand?	Since when?
Il y a ...?	Is there/are there ...?
Combien de ...?	How much ...? How many ...?
Depuis combien de temps ...?	For how long ...?
C'est combien?	How much is it?
Comment?	How?
Où?	Where?
Pourquoi?	Why?
Qu'est-ce que? / **Que?**	What?
Quel?	Which?

- Learn these **three easy ways** of forming questions.

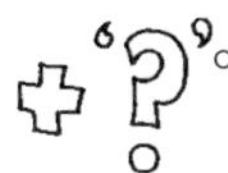

◦ **Easy way 1**

Add a question mark and raise your voice at the end.

- **Vous aimez les glaces.**
  You like ice cream
- **Vous aimez les glaces?**
  Do you like ice cream?

◦ **Easy way 2**

The magic phrase **est-ce que** changes a sentence into a question. All you need to do is place it before your sentence. Then, when speaking, raise your voice at the end; when writing, remember to add a question mark at the end. For example:

- **La gare est en face du cinéma.**
  The station is opposite the cinema.
  Est-ce que la gare est en face du cinéma?
  Is the station opposite the cinema?
- **Il y a une piscine au centre sportif.**
  There is a swimming-pool at the sports centre.
  Est-ce qu'il y a une piscine au centre sportif?
  Is there a swimming-pool at the sports centre?

Note the apostrophe in the second example. Remember: **que** becomes **qu'** before a vowel.

◦ **Easy way 3**

Reversing a verb makes a sentence into a simple question. For example:

- **Tu vas au collège.**
  You go to school.
  Vas-tu au collège?
  Are you going to school?
- **Vous avez fait vos devoirs.**
  You have done your homework.
  Avez-vous fait vos devoirs?
  Have you done your homework?

- Have at hand groups of questions relevant to specific topics and **learn them!** Here are some to get you started:

◦ **Personal Information**

- **Comment t'appelles-tu?**
  What's your name?
- **Où habites-tu?**
  Where do you live?
- **Est-ce que tu as des frères ou des soeurs?**
  Do you have any brothers or sisters?
- **Tu as des animaux à la maison?**
  Do you have any pets?

◦ **House/Home**

- **Tu habites dans une maison ou dans un appartement?**
  Do you live in a house or a flat?
- **Comment est ta maison?**
  What is your house like?
- **Il y a combien de pièces dans ta maison?**
  How many rooms are there in your house?
- **Depuis combien de temps est-ce que tu habites dans cette maison?**
  For how long have you been staying in this house?

◦ **Free time/Leisure**

- **Qu'est-ce que tu fais comme passe-temps?**
  What are your hobbies?
- **Quel est ton sport préféré?**
  What is your favourite sport?
- **Est-ce qu'il y a beaucoup de distractions dans ta ville?**
  Are there lots of things to do in your town?
- **Combien de temps est-ce que tu passes à regarder la télé?**
  How much time do you spend watching television?

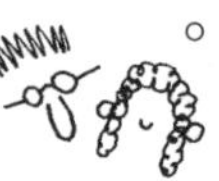

Descriptions

- **Tu connais ...?**
  Do you know ...?
- **Est-ce qu'il est grand ou petit?**
  Is he tall or small?
- **Il a les cheveux de quelle couleur?**
  What colour is his hair?
- **Il porte des lunettes?**
  Does he wear glasses?

Work/Future Plans

- **Tu as un travail à mi-temps?**
  Do you have a part-time job?
- **Comment est le travail?**
  What is the work like?
- **Tu gagnes combien d'argent?**
  How much money do you earn?
- **Qu'est-ce que tu veux faire comme travail quand tu auras quitté l'école?**
  What sort of work do you want to do when you leave school?

Home-town

- **Où habites-tu? C'est une ville ou un village?**
  Where do you live? Is it a town or a village?
- **Où se trouve ...?**
  Where is ... situated?
- **Qu'est-ce qu'on peut faire à ...?**
  What can you do in ...?
- **Est-ce qu'il y a de bons magasins?**
  Are there good shops?

Daily Routine

- **Tu te lèves à quelle heure?**
  When do you get up?
- **Qu'est-ce que tu prends pour le petit déjeuner?**
  What do you have for breakfast?
- **Comment est-ce que tu vas à l'école?**
  How do you go to school?
- **Que fais-tu le soir?**
  What do you do in the evening?

Holidays – Present and Immediate Future

- **Où est-ce que tu vas en vacances cette année?**
  Where are you going on holiday this year?
- **Où est-ce que tu vas loger?**
  Where are you going to stay?
- **Combien de temps est-ce que tu vas y passer?**
  How long are you going to spend there?
- **Qu'est-ce que tu vas faire à ...?**
  What are you going to do in ...?

Holidays – Past

- **Où est-ce que tu es allé(e) en vacances l'année dernière?**
  Where did you go on holiday last year?
- **Où as-tu logé?**
  Where did you stay?
- **Combien de temps est-ce que tu y as passé?**
  How long did you spend there?
- **Qu'est-ce que tu as fait?**
  What did you do?

Weather and Time

- **Quel temps fait-il?**
  What's the weather like?
- **Quelle heure est-il?**
  What time is it?
- **À quelle heure ...?**
  At what time...?
- **C'est quand, ton anniversaire?**
  When is your birthday?

Questions for help!

- **Est-ce que tu peux parler plus lentement, s'il te plaît?**
  Can you speak more slowly please?
- **Peux-tu répéter la question, s'il te plaît?**
  Can you repeat the question please?
- **Qu'est-ce que tu veux dire?**
  What do you mean?
- **Comment ça s'écrit?**
  How do you spell that?

Now listen to these question words, phrases and sentences on pages 44–47 spoken in **section ten** of the tape. Repeat each one aloud as you hear it.

Many of the questions above use the familiar word for you – **tu**. You may need or may want to use the polite form – **vous**, instead. Remember that **tu** is used for a person you know well, e.g. a member of your family or a friend. **Vous** is used for a person you don't know well, or a group of people. Usually, if you call someone by their first name, you would use **tu**; if you call somebody 'Mr' or 'Mrs', you would use **vous**.

Now try exercises 46 and 47.

Exercise 46

1. Replace **tu** with **vous** in the questions on pages 45–47 above. Check the section on verbs on pages 38–42 for the proper endings if you need to.
2. Now make up answers to all of your questions. This will help prepare you for both Speaking and General Writing.

Exercise 47

Here is a list of question words and phrases and a selection of sentence endings.
Combine these question words and phrases with a suitable ending. (The topic is 'school'.)

Question Words and Phrases	*Endings*
Tu peux me parler de ...	**... est-ce que tu vas à cette école?**
Tu peux décrire ...	**... se trouve l'école?**
Comment ...	**... élèves à l'école?**
Qui ...	**... est ta matière préférée?**
Quand ...	**... est-ce que tu passes à faire tes devoirs?**
Il y a combien d' ...	**... est-ce que les cours commencent et finissent?**
Combien de cours ...	**... tu aimes cette matière?**
Combien de temps ...	**... est ton prof favori?**
Comment est-ce que ...	**... ton collège?**
Où ...	**... tu penses de l'école en général?**
Depuis quand ...	**... ton trajet de la maison à l'école?**
Quelle (Quel) ...	**... est-ce que tu as par jour?**
Pourquoi est-ce que ...	**... s'appelle ton école?**
Qu'est-ce que ...	**... tu vas à l'école?**

Answers and translations are on page 48. (You may have selected other endings which are also correct – check them with your teacher.)

It's important to learn questions as well as answers. Using questions shows initiative. This will get you a good grade for Speaking and will help you with General Level Writing.

Impressive phrases

Do you want to write impressive French? Do you want to be able to read, listen and understand more complicated French? Then have a list of impressive phrases at hand. Here are some to get you started:

- **avant de + infinitive**

e.g.	avant de manger	before eating
	avant de partir	before leaving
	avant de lire	before reading

- **sans + infinitive**

e.g.	sans rester	without staying
	sans finir	without finishing
	sans comprendre	without understanding

- **pour + infinitive**

e.g.	pour trouver	in order to find
	pour choisir	in order to choose
	pour descendre	in order to go downstairs

- **en ______ant**

e.g.	en attendant	while waiting
	en choisissant	while choosing

- **après avoir + past participle**

  e.g. après avoir donné/vendu/fini/vu
  after having given/sold/finished/seen

- **après être + past participle**

  e.g. après être allé(e)(s), ...
  after having gone, ...
  après être parti(e)(s), ...
  after having left, ...

Throughout your Standard Grade course, work on the following exercise.

Exercise 48

Make your own list of impressive phrases and keep adding to it.

Answers and translation

Exercise 47

Tu peux me parler de ton trajet de la maison à l'école?	Can you tell me about your journey from home to school?
Tu peux décrire ton collège?	Can you describe your school?
Comment s'appelle ton école?	What's the name of your school?
Qui est ton prof favori?	Who is your favourite teacher?
Quand est-ce que les cours commencent et finissent?	When do lessons start and finish?
Il y a combien d'élèves à l'école?	How many pupils are at the school?
Combien de cours est-ce que tu as par jour?	How many classes do you have each day?
Combien de temps est-ce que tu passes à faire tes devoirs?	How much time do you spend doing your homework?
Comment est-ce que tu vas à l'école?	How do you get to school?
Où se trouve l'école?	Where is the school situated?
Depuis quand est-ce que tu vas à cette école?	Since when have you been going to this school?
Quelle est ta matière préférée?	What is your favourite subject?
Pourquoi est-ce que tu aimes cette matière?	Why do you like that subject?
Qu'est-ce que tu penses de l'école en général?	What do you think of school in general?

Et bonne chance!

Printed by Inglis Allen, Kirkcaldy